Philippe

The Black Sheep

For my favorite lambs — Jonas, Thomas, Dimitri, Frederic, Manuel, Jerome, and Nastya

Library of Congress Control Number: 2015958233
ISBN: 978-0-916754-45-7

Printed and bound in France
The text of this book is set in the Baskerville family; titles are set in ITC Coolman, Std.
The art was executed in pen and ink/Gouache.
Art direction and design: Bryan Canniff
Edit: George Held
Tech: Gary Osius

Filsinger & Company, Ltd.
www.filsingerco.com

First Edition 10 9 8 7 6 5 4 3 2 1

Pulsio - Paris, France and Sofia, Bulgaria
02/2016 - run 1:12213

Philippe
The Black Sheep

by Joan Dupont

pictures by Ellen Shire

Filsinger & Company, Ltd.
New York, New York

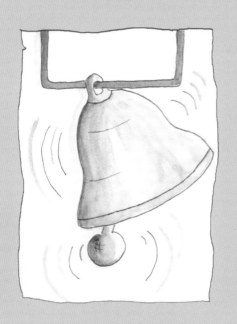

This is the story
of Philippe, of France,
a Salt Marsh Lamb
with artistic ambitions.

He longs to escape
to Mont Saint-Michel,
to avoid a lamb's fate
and paint under its bell.

Across the blue bay
from Mont Saint-Michel,
the famed sheep of France
prance, graze, and swell.

When tides are low,
the flocks do feast
on salty grass
that makes tasty meat...

for the joy of the French,
who love to eat.

When waters rise,
the flocks run fleet
to high safe hills
to huddle and bleat

...until they are sent
for their final "sleep."

But then there's **Philippe**,
the blackest of sheep...

"I was not born
for this life of breeding,
the nights of fear,
the days of feeding,

"to tremble and hide
at the turn of the tide.

"I'm not a mere sheep
who follows the pack,
but a talented artist
on the run from the axe."

So Philippe built a raft,
a sea-worthy craft,
where he painted the towers
of Mont Saint-Michel

until all hours,
while his family glowered:

"Philippe doesn't eat."
"Philippe doesn't sleep."
"Philippe thinks he's way
too smart for a sheep."

8

One night, on that raft,
named the *Mont Saint-Michel,*
the winds became stormy,
the sea began to swell.

The moon brightened,
the sky lightened.
The waves heightened,
Philippe was frightened.

Philippe once fearless,
Philippe once free,
Philippe was now floating
far out to sea.

He clung to the rope,
feet braced to the deck,
the waves overlapped him,
and threatened a wreck.

Our hero was drenched
when he finally reached shore,
his wet wool blacker,
heart bleaker than before.

9

From high in the air,
came the peal of a bell,
and out from the mist
rose Mont Saint-Michel.

And what did he see,
while wading to land?
Not grassy sheep country,
but tricky quicksand.

Philippe, the pilgrim,
then kissed the shore.
He ran up the hill,
he ran past the stores.

His eye, keen and eager,
passed over the roofs.
He sped up the steps
on his hard little hoofs.

"Oh, love of my life,
land of my dreams!
How lovely, how bright
now everything seems!"

11

"Never," he mused,
"did I ever care
about food that I ate
when I lived over there.

He saw a bistro,
sat down for an omelette
and after that-o
some greens and tomato.

Some white wine, dry,
and a bite of *brie,*
and the chef's rich cake,
a renowned specialty.

"Here, it's the mood,
or is it the height,
that suddenly gives me
a grand appetite?"

At the restaurant
was a red-headed lady
they all called "Tante" —
she was *très charmante*.

She came to his side
and whispered in his ear,
"I see you have good taste.
Pray, what brought you here?"

"My ship," said Philippe
"is stranded on your shores.
I've become a stray sheep
who would gladly clean floors.

"An artist by profession,
I am in love with beauty,
but I'll do what I can,
I will do my duty."

"Dear Sir," said Tante,
while shedding a tear,
"I wish you'd stay here,
where your company would cheer...

13

"For my days go by sadly,
my bistro does badly,
and I tremble at the rule
of Chef Louis the Cruel.

"But alas, I'm afraid,
all I can offer
is the lowliest job,
a simple dishwasher."

"Madame," cried Philippe,
"may I call you Tante?
It's all I could wish for,
all I could want.

"I've never washed dishes,
but I'll give it a try,
and your every last plate
shall be scrubbed and then dried."

The two hugged each other
quickly and tight.
"To work," said Philippe,
"I'll start tonight!"

14

But down in the kitchen,
all was not well.
The fridge it was dirty
and gave off a bad smell.

The pots were unwashed,
neglected for weeks.
The floor was a mess,
and the faucets had leaks.

The walls they were cracked,
paint faded and peeling.
The table'd been hacked,
and food spattered the ceiling!

Louis the chef,
a ferocious fellow,
brandished long knives,
and flashed teeth stained yellow.

He ate so much
it gave him a pain.
But what he liked best
was to loudly complain.

15

When he saw Philippe,
he let out a yelp.
"Is this," he jeered,
"what they sent me as help?

"A juicy little lamb,
much better than pork.
I would love him stuck
on the tines of my fork!

"Let's have potluck.
How 'bout it, my pet?
Old Louis will cook
what you'll never forget!"

Philippe's heart quaked,
but he had to keep calm:
"If I do my work well,
he will do me no harm."

16

So every day
Philippe was up early,
washing away
as Louis watched, surly.

Soon there was not
a dish in the sink.
And all of the kitchen
looked span and spic.

"Bah!" cried Louis,
"the day's just begun.
Don't think you can go
for a stroll in the sun!

"There are pea pods to shell,
greens to rinse and to dry,
onions to peel
and you'd better not cry."

"I think," said the chef,
"it's time for a drop
of something to drink —
and for me, a lamb chop.

"Looking at you makes me
too hungry to shop,
so YOU — go to market —
at a fast even trot.

So Philippe did those chores,
and Louis was maddened
that not for a moment
was our black sheep saddened.

He polished the silver,
with his wool made it shine.
He licked 40 labels
for 40 bottles of wine.

"We need kilos of spuds,
and twenty of cheese,
and ten tubs of butter,
and a million small peas

"and pots of rich cream
and dozens of eggs.
Go quick as you can
on your spindly black legs."

Back to the kitchen
he went, feeling faint.
Down in that dungeon
was no place to paint.

'Twas no day for dreaming,
for beneath his great weight,
Louis was screaming,
"You loafer, you're late...

"I have lunch to fix
for twenty at least,
and if no one shows up,
then I'll have me a feast.

Though the breeze blew sweet,
and the sun shone strong,
Philippe's heart felt heavy,
as his shadow grew long.

And though he whistled,
to keep spirits light,
Saint-Michel's towers
seemed far out of sight.

"So come down from the clouds,
and no tricks from you!
You'd better get busy
or I might fix you!"

20

The church bell struck one,
then a quarter past.
"Ho ho!" said Louis,
"this is too good to last!"

Not a soul at one thirty,
or at a quarter to...
"Well, well," grinned Louis,
"only one thing to do."

At two o'clock,
he made a loud toast:
"Long live Chef Louis!"
and he ate all the roast.

By two thirty-five,
he'd gobbled the peas,
ten heads of lettuce,
the tenderest cheese.

21

And after he'd eaten
the heart of the tart,
came the ring of Tante's bell,
which gave him a start.

"What luck, my good cook,
we're saved, take a look —

"guests by the dozens,
all coming to us,
the glorious bunch
on that blue Mont Tours bus."

22

But Louis looked ill
and had turned quite yellow.
He gasped hard for breath,
the poor old fellow.

The tyrant's tart tongue
turned almost to stone.
When he tried to yell,
out came a groan!

"There is no more food,
we're down to the bone!
Oh my fame, my honor…"
He let out a moan.

"Take over, Philippe,
I count on you, Sheep."
With a sigh and a belch,
the chef fell asleep.

Philippe clambered upstairs
to explain the mishap.
"I'm afraid, dear Tante,
Louis' taking a nap.

"Our mad chef has cooked
up his own Waterloo:
he prepared a repast
but devoured it too."

This news left the lady
tearing her hair...
but Philippe moved fast,
at once everywhere.

Stirring soup on a burner,
flipping jacks in the air;
he ran up and down
the kitchen's long stair.

Nobody knew
how Philippe got it done,
but upstairs and downstairs,
there was feasting and fun.

"That lamb has a way
of presenting a plate!
Who knows what it was,
what it was that we ate?

"Never tasted a dish
like that one before!
Take our word, dearest lady,
we'll be back for much more!"

And all the while,
Louis lay on the floor.
When the last guest had left,
he let out a big snore.

25

Tante worried and hurried
to call the M.D.
He rolled Louis over,
and said, "Let me see...

"But tell me, dear lady,
is he always so yellow?"
"YELLOW?" yelled Louis,
in a *basso profundo*.

"Yes," said the doc, "quite so.
"You're perfectly yellow
from your head to your toe,
and that is, I might add,
a long way to go!

"But please do not fret,
the yellow won't stay.
It's just that rich food
wastes your liver away.

"So, no more cream,
and sauces won't do,
and no more lamb,
not even in stew."

While Chef Louis thought
of the meals he must miss,
the doc wrote a list
of what must be bought:

Lotions and potions
and little blue pills,
bitter to the taste
but good for his ills.

"All that weight on his feet
is rather a risk.
I'd give him a seat
and a giant egg whisk."

"Oh, good," said Tante,
his omelettes are the best."
"And I," said Philippe,
"will do all the rest."

27

So Louis sat on his fat
while all came to look
at Mont Saint-Michel's
monumentalist cook.

Louis whisking his whites
was the greatest of sights,
but the biggest of treats
was watching him eat.

He's served diet greens,
and very dry beans,
without cream or butter...
and he doesn't mutter.

The meat it is lean,
the biscuits sans flour,
and the yogurt he gets
is completely sour.

And when the old chef
has eaten his fill,
the sheep serves Louis
a bitter blue pill.

Tante was so pleased
to see her bistro grow
thanks to Philippe,
who ran the whole show.

28

But then, one morning,
when the tides were low,
Philippe's raft vanished
as did our hero.

Everyone feared
he was lost at sea,
that their dear Philippe
was no more to be,

when out of the blue
from across the bay,
a small boat bobbed,
heading their way!

While dear Tante sobbed,
the crowd cheered merrily:
"It's our Philippe
and his whole family!"

29

At first they appeared
a little bit shy,
which was, no doubt,
the reason why —

to make sure that the sheep
had no cause for alarm,
the villagers acted
gentle and warm.

And before very long,
by listening and looking,
Philippe's mother and sister
learned the finest of cooking.

But Philippe was not free
until a while later
when his father became
a perfect headwaiter.

30

Now every day,
Philippe steals away.
He leaps up the street,
he runs in the sun,

and under the bell,
among the flowers,
Philippe paints the towers
of the Mont Saint-Michel.

The End